ANIMALS AT

SNOW LEOPARDS IN DANGER

BY SOFIA MAIMONE

Gareth Stevens
Publishing

Please visit our website, www.garethstevens.com. For a free color catalog of all our high-quality books, call toll free 1-800-542-2595 or fax 1-877-542-2596.

Library of Congress Cataloging-in-Publication Data

Snow leopards in danger / by Sofia Maimone.
       p. cm. – (Animals at risk)
Includes index.
ISBN 978-1-4339-9175-2 (pbk.)
ISBN 978-1-4339-9176-9 (6-Pack)
ISBN 978-1-4339-9174-5 (library binding)
1. Snow leopard — Juvenile literature. 2. Endangered species — Juvenile literature. I. Maimone, Sofia Z. II. Title.
QL737.C23 M35 2014
599.75'55—dc23

First Edition

Published in 2014 by
Gareth Stevens Publishing
111 East 14th Street, Suite 349
New York, NY 10003

Copyright © 2014 Gareth Stevens Publishing

Designer: Andrea Davison-Bartolotta
Editor: Therese M. Shea

Photo credits: Cover, pp. 1, 15, 16, 19 iStockphoto/Thinkstock; p. 5 Andy Poole/Shutterstock.com; p. 6 Mike Rogal/Shutterstock.com; p. 7 Bernhard Richter/Shutterstock.com; pp. 8, 18 Photos.com/Thinkstock; p. 9 Altrendo Nature/Getty Images; p. 10 (left) Andreas Resch/Shutterstock.com, (right) KimPinPhotography/Shutterstock.com; p. 11 Joseph Van Os/Stockbyte/Getty Images; p. 12 Dietmar Heinz/Picture Press/Getty Images; p. 13 belizar/Shutterstock.com; p. 17 Stayer/Shutterstock.com; p. 20 Samuel R. Maglione/Photo Researchers/Getty Images; p. 21 (borders) ildogesto/Shutterstock.com, (map) Arid Ocean/Shutterstock.com.

Printed in the United States of America

CPSIA compliance information: Batch #CS13GS: For further information contact Gareth Stevens, New York, New York at 1-800-542-2595.

CONTENTS

Words in the glossary appear in **bold** type the first time they are used in the text.

CATS OF MYSTERY

Snow leopards are big cats that live only in the mountains of central Asia. Much of their life is a mystery because they're so hard to spot in their **habitat**. Some ancient stories said snow leopards could change shape to hide from people!

In real life, it seems like that. People who live near snow leopards say they just appear and then quickly disappear again. Sadly, snow leopards might really disappear from Earth for good. They're **endangered**.

WILD FACTS
Snow leopards are found in just 12 countries in Asia.

▼ There are just a few thousand snow leopards left. We mostly learn about them through zoos.

Heavy Fur Coat

Snow leopards' coats make them hard to spot. They're mostly gray with black markings. This is perfect **camouflage** for the big cats' rocky homes. Their coats are very thick, too, which helps them stay warm in extremely cold conditions. Snow leopards even have fur on the bottom of their paws.

Unfortunately, this beautiful fur is one of the reasons snow leopards are endangered. Hunters kill them and sell their fur. It's used to make coats and rugs.

Illegal hunters, called poachers, have put the snow leopard population in danger.

SUPER JUMPERS

Snow leopards are well suited for mountain life because they're excellent jumpers. They can leap from a cliff to a narrow **ledge** with ease. They've been known to jump as far as 50 feet (15 m)! The snow leopard's long tail helps it keep balance.

Snow leopards have been seen as high as 18,000 feet (5.5 km) above sea level. It's no wonder they're rarely seen in the wild. It's hard for people to even breathe in such high places.

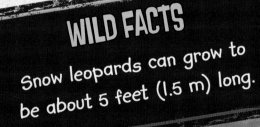

WILD FACTS
Snow leopards can grow to be about 5 feet (1.5 m) long.

A snow leopard's tail may add an extra 3 feet (90 cm) to its length.

CARNIVORE!

Snow leopards use their leaping skills to catch dinner. They're mostly meat eaters, or carnivores. They hunt mountain animals, such as sheep, goats, birds, and **marmots**.

Snow leopards eat slowly. They might eat **prey** over 3 or 4 days. They guard their meal and keep other animals, such as vultures, from taking it.

A snow leopard hunts a large animal every 8 to 10 days. It has no fear about hunting animals three times its weight, such as **yaks**!

MARMOT

YAK

▼ Like other big cats, snow leopards sneak up on their prey.

HIDDEN FAMILIES

Snow leopards live alone. They mark their territory with scratches in the ground and their **scent**. These things mean "stay away." However, between January and March, they look for a **mate**.

A mother snow leopard has two or three cubs in June or July. She takes care of them by herself in a hidden den. She begins to teach them to hunt when they're about 3 months old. Cubs stay with their mother for about a year and a half.

WILD FACTS
How hidden is a snow leopard den? Scientists had never found one before 2012!

Snow leopard cubs don't open their eyes until a week after they're born.

HUNGRY CATS

In winter months, animals like marmots go into their underground homes and won't come out until spring. When snow leopards can't find enough prey, they travel down from the mountains.

Sometimes the prey they find is livestock. People with large herds of animals, such as yaks and horses, need a lot of grassy land for their animals. These lands are sometimes at the foot of the mountains that are the snow leopards' habitat. Herders may fight snow leopards by killing or poisoning them.

WILD FACTS
Mountain **mining** is another reason snow leopards leave their habitat.

Adult snow leopards usually have light green or gray eyes.

Much of the year, life in the mountains is cold. Snow leopards need to eat whatever they can find to stay alive. This may be why snow leopards eat more grass and plants than other big cats. They need the **nutrients**.

Snow leopards live about 22 years in zoos. Life in the wild is much harder, so they probably don't live as long. They're always on the move looking for prey. One scientist tracked a snow leopard. It traveled 27 miles (43 km) in a single night!

WILD FACTS
Snow leopards don't roar. They yowl!

▼ A snow leopard's thick coat helps it stay alive in tough conditions.

A FEW THOUSAND

There may only be 4,000 snow leopards left in the wild today. Although there are laws against killing snow leopards, it's often hard to make people follow these laws. Snow leopard fur is so valued that poachers are willing to take the chance of punishment.

Herders make more money by increasing their livestock and their land. This means less land for snow leopards to find prey. Some organizations are working to teach herders better ways to deal with snow leopards on their lands.

Snow leopard body parts are used in Chinese **medicine**.

SAVE THE GHOST CAT!

Snow leopards are sometimes called "ghosts of the mountains" or "ghost cats." You might be able to spot one, but blink...and it's gone!

Most of the snow leopard habitat lies within China's borders, so much of the efforts to help the big cats are being focused there. Snow leopards need land and prey to hunt. They need people to save them from poachers. With a little help, these "ghost cats" can continue to live mysterious lives high up in the mountains.

The Snow Leopard's Habitat

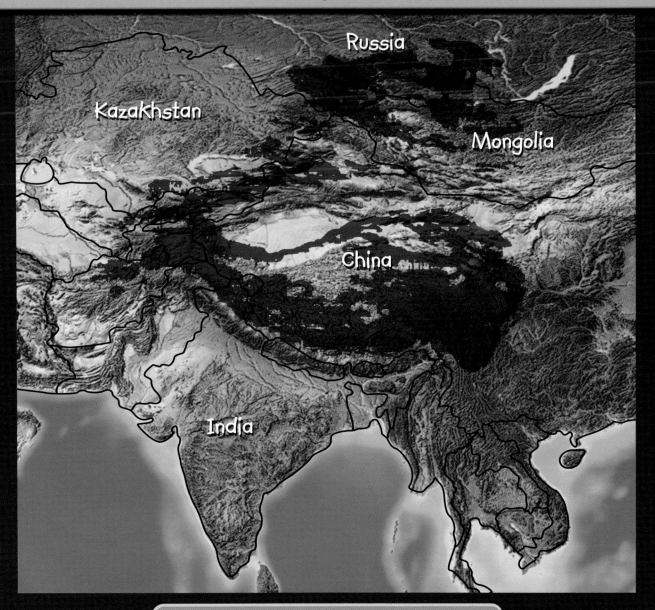

The total snow leopard habitat is about the size of Mexico.

GLOSSARY

camouflage: colors or shapes of animals that allow them to blend with their surroundings

endangered: in danger of dying out

habitat: the natural place where an animal or plant lives

ledge: a rock shelf

marmot: a brownish animal related to squirrels that lives on the ground and in underground dens

mate: one of two animals that come together to produce babies

medicine: a drug taken to make a sick person well

mining: having to do with digging something out of the ground

nutrient: something a living thing needs to grow and stay alive

prey: an animal hunted by other animals for food

scent: a smell

yak: a large, long-haired ox with curved horns

FOR MORE INFORMATION

BOOKS

Montgomery, Sy. *Saving the Ghost of the Mountain: An Expedition Among Snow Leopards in Mongolia.* Boston, MA: Houghton Mifflin Books for Children, 2009.

Scherer, Glenn, and Marty Fletcher. *The Snow Leopard: Help Save This Endangered Species!* Berkeley Heights, NJ: Enslow Publishers, 2008.

WEBSITES

Mammals: Snow Leopard
www.sandiegozoo.org/animalbytes/t-snow_leopard.html
Want to hear what a snow leopard sounds like? Check out this website!

Snow Leopards for Kids
www.snowleopardconservancy.org/kids/text/kids.htm
Find out what kids are doing to save snow leopards.

Snow Leopard Trust
www.snowleopard.org
Read much more about the threats facing snow leopards and what people are doing to help.

INDEX